Duck Socks

Written and illustrated by
An Vrombaut

Collins

Hip has duck socks.

Hip has red dot socks.

Hop has duck socks ...

red dots and no dots.

Hop is a sad duck.

Hip gets a red sack.

Hop digs up a sock ...

a red dot sock!

Hop has red dot socks.

Red dot socks rock!

/h/

15

🐾 Review: After reading 🐾

Use your assessment from hearing the children read to choose any GPCs, words or tricky words that need additional practice.

Read 1: Decoding

- Point to the word **Duck** on the front cover. Model sounding it out, d/u/ck, and blending the sounds together. Ask the children to sound out and blend the words **socks** (page 2), **sack** (page 7) and **rock** (page 13). Ensure the children understand that the two letters "ck" make one sound.
- Look at the "I spy sounds" pages (14–15). Say the sounds together. How many items can the children spot with the /r/ sound in them? (e.g. *red, robot, rainbow, rabbit, rocket, rocking horse, rat*)
- How many words can they spot with the /h/ sound in them? (e.g. *horse, hat, helmet, hippo, hopscotch, helicopter, house*)

Read 2: Prosody

- Model reading each page with expression to the children. After you have read each page, ask the children to have a go at reading with expression.

Read 3: Comprehension

- For every question ask the children how they know the answer. Ask:
  - Why was Hop a sad duck? (*his socks were odd – one spotted and one plain*)
  - What do you think Hip said to Hop when he was sad? (e.g. *"Don't be sad, I can help."*)
  - How did Hip help Hop? (*he brought a sack of socks*)
  - Do you think Hop was happy by the end of the story? Why? (*yes, he had a pair of spotted socks – just like Hip*)